True or False?

Transportation

Daniel Nunn

Raintree
Chicago, Illinois

© 2013 Raintree
an imprint of Capstone Global Library, LLC
Chicago, Illinois

To contact Capstone Global Library please phone 800-747-4992, or visit our website www.capstonepub.com

All rights reserved. No part of this publication may be reproduced or transmitted in any form or by any means, electronic or mechanical, including photocopying, recording, taping, or any information storage and retrieval system, without permission in writing from the publisher.

Edited by Dan Nunn, Rebecca Rissman, and Catherine Veitch
Designed by Joanna Hinton-Malivoire
Picture research by Ruth Blair
Production by Victoria Fitzgerald
Originated by Capstone Global Library

Library of Congress Cataloging-in-Publication Data
Nunn, Daniel.
True or False? Transportation / Daniel Nunn.
pages cm.—(True or false?)
Includes bibliographical references and index.
ISBN 978-1-4109-5069-7 (hb)
ISBN 978-1-4109-5075-8 (pb)
1. Transportation—Miscellanea—Juvenile literature. I. Title.
TA1149.N86 2013
388—dc23 2012019713

Acknowledgments
We would like to thank the following for permission to reproduce photographs: iStockphoto pp. 16 (© Kovacs dr. Robert), 18 (© studioworxx); Shutterstock pp. 4 (© Maksim Toome, © Mat Hayward, © best images, © hfng), 5 and back cover (© Kosarev Alexander, © M. Unal Ozmen), 6 (© Minerva Studio), 7 and back cover (© Michal Jurkowski, © Nagy Jozsef - Attila), 8 (© Roman Gorielov), 9 (© Petr Student, © cherezoff), 10 (© Isabel FernÃ¡ndez FernÃ¡ndez), 11 (© Pablo Scapinachis), 12 (© MC_PP), 13 (© DinoZ), 14 (© Netfalls - Remy Musser), 15 (© Kalmatsuy Tatyana), 17 (© Eric Isselée, © cynoclub), 19 (© Marcel Mooij), 20 (© sonya etchison), 21 (© risteski goce, © Khoroshunova Olga), 22 (© 1971yes).

Cover photographs reproduced with permission of Shutterstock (© Eric Isselée (hippo), © cynoclub (child)).

Every effort has been made to contact copyright holders of any material reproduced in this book. Any omissions will be rectified in subsequent printings if notice is given to the publisher.

Printed in the United States 5488

Contents

Transportation 4
Cars 5
Trains 7
Buses 9
Planes 11
Ships 13
Bicycles 15
Animals 17
Balloons 19
Submarines 21
Can You Remember? 23
Index, Activity 24

Transportation

People use transportation to get around. How much do **YOU** know about different forms of transportation?

Cars

Some cars run on ice cream instead of gasoline.

True or false?

✕ False!

Most cars run on gasoline.

Trains

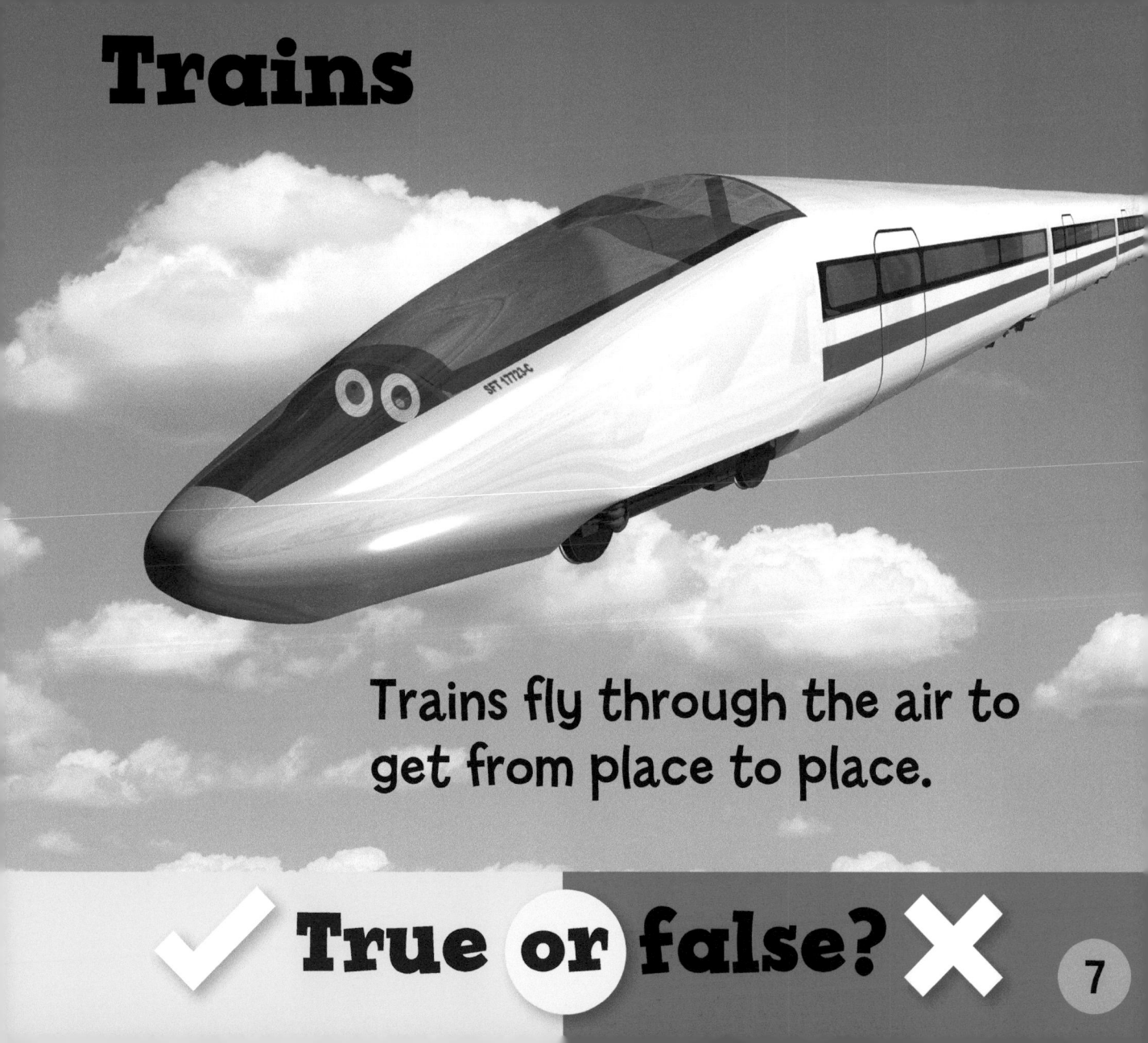

Trains fly through the air to get from place to place.

True or false?

✗ False!

Trains travel on the ground, not in the air! They move along special rails called railroad tracks.

Buses

All buses have a roof.

True or false?

✗ False!

Some buses do not have a roof. Tour buses do not have a roof. People ride in them to see the sights.

Planes

Planes have wings instead of wheels.

True or false?

✗ False!

Planes have wings AND wheels. Planes need their wheels for taking off and landing.

Ships

Some boats move using the wind.

True or false?

True!

Some boats move using the wind.
They catch the wind with giant sails.

Bicycles

All bicycles have two wheels the same size.

True or false?

✗ False!

This bike has one big wheel and one little wheel. It is called a penny-farthing!

Animals

Some people use animals to get around.

True or false?

True!

Some people use animals to get around. Some horses pull people in carriages.

Balloons

Some people use balloons to fly from place to place.

True or false?

True!

Some people fly using giant hot air balloons. The people stand in a basket underneath the balloon.

Submarines

Some vehicles can travel under water.

True or false?

True!

Some vehicles can travel under water. These special boats are called submarines.

Can You Remember?

Which vehicle has wheels and wings?

Which vehicle moves using the wind?

Which vehicle can travel under water?

Look back through the book to check your answers.

Index

air 7, 8
carriages 18
gasoline 5, 6
railroad tracks 8
roof 9, 10
sails 14
water 21, 22, 23
wind 13, 14, 23
wings 11, 12, 23
wheels 11, 12, 15, 16, 23

Activity

Make Your Own True or False Game
Help your child make a Transportation: True or False game. Collect a selection of pictures of transportation from magazines. Mount each picture on cardboard. Then with the child, write a series of true or false statements about the transportation in the pictures, on separate pieces of cardboard. Put one statement with each corresponding picture. On the back of each picture, write if the statement is true or false. For the game, read the statement out loud, ask the child if it is true or false, then have the child turn over the picture to check if he or she is correct. To extend the activity, ask the child to write the statements and whether they are true or false, and then ask you the questions.